CW00690691

Extras . . .

Poetry purely words

Music merely notes

Art we perceive . . .

Each exotic, esoteric

Merged — Matched, Magical

Enjoy with Extras . . .

by
Alan Reavill

EXTRAS . . .

Extras. . . is a collection of poems most of which were not included in the earlier 'This is not a Cricket Book' series: The title being the only connection!

Consisting of writing mostly carried out during the last two years; 'Extras' includes some favourites which did not accord with the themes of the series. It contains six poems and references related to Ilkeston and Derbyshire where I was born and educated. Art and Music, often related, are also frequently referenced.

'The Evening Sky'; published previously is included as an introduction to the 'Study-Window Art' collection which concludes the book and is a "Work in progress" project for the Arts Society.

I sincerely hope that you are entertained and enjoy this anthology.

THIS IS NOT A CRICKET BOOK!

Extras © Sept 2021 by Alan Reavill.

All rights reserved. No part of this book may be reproduced in any form or by any electronic or mechanical means including information storage and retrieval systems, without permission in writing from the author. The only exception is by a reviewer, who may quote short excerpts in a review.
This book is a work of fiction. Names, characters, places, and incidents either are products of the author's imagination or are used fictitiously. Any resemblance to actual persons, living or dead, events, or locales is entirely coincidental.

First Published: Sept 2021
by
Budding Authors Assistant
www.help2publish.co.uk

ISBN: 9781919625416

DEDICATION

Dedicated with sincere thanks to Margaret, who has tolerated varied and numerous mood swings along my recent writing sojourn . . . and those pre-writing years.

Additionally to friends and others, who unwittingly or not, provided material, support and encouragement, which assisted my writings.

.

Contents

Notes

MEMORIES

I have read . . . or heard it said . . . or perhaps it was a dream . . .
That, as a man grows old his memory is beset.
All too often, with doubts and sad regret.
And thoughts of what might have been . . .

Of ill remembered, half forgotten dreams and schemes.
Places, scenes, childhood bliss, growing up . . . and that first,
   romantic kiss.
Of friends, holidays, work - achievements and colleagues
   he now will miss.
But perhaps the past, nor life ahead, are exactly as they seem.

For how times change: childhood memories and dreams do not fade.
But may now appear foolish, too ambitious,
   unlikely to be achieved.
Were they ever realistic? Could they ever have been believed?
Yes . . . 'The best laid schemes of mice and men' -
   were sometimes made.

Looking back, we can all excuse our lack of decision,
   of clear vision . . .
But doubts from such thoughts will grow -
   fester as we ponder . . .
Will inevitably seem . . . ill founded - just silly . . .
   But, we will wonder . . .
As a man grows old . . . he will rethink . . .
Question in his mind that decision . . .
And ask that question . . .
What might have been . . .?

1

Notes

PHILOSOPHICAL GOLD

"I think, therefore I am . . ."

So perhaps I should consider who . . . what . . . and why . . .?

But . . . not easy this story to unfold.

Nor any reason that it needs to be told . . .

Other than, as a would be poet . . . I should try!

I came late to this subject called Philosophy . . .

As, perchance I did to poetic writing too.

Descartes gives me the obvious cue

And so, perhaps, for now, it's farewell, to Topography

Who? A Grammar School lad - Maths and Science led . . .

But . . . No time, or interest in poetry and of Art . . .

Don't recall any reference or talk of Descartes . . .

Nothing to indicate the interests which lay ahead.

What? Well, no obvious pattern or plan: A lack of ambition . . .?

Save, perhaps, success in sport if truth be told.

How many runs, wickets . . . maiden overs bowled . . .

The Arts . . . Literature . . . Poetry . . .

Sadly . . . still an omission.

Why? The question every philosopher must ask . . .

When? Why? The change I cannot begin to explain . . .

But . . . Now I write . . . I think . . . therefore . . . I am!

Literature is now my domain.

Thank You Mr Descartes . . .

In Poetry I strive to explain . . . To remove the mask.

Notes

ILKESTON

Ilkeston - Perhaps not the Rose of our beautiful County -
   but fully deserving of a Crown!
A changed, ever changing - but proud, wonderful town.
From Ancient Times, Doomesday Book, Danelaw farming
through Royal Charter to thriving present day.
Textiles, Coal Mining, Iron and Steel . . . a varied array.

St Mary's Church: understated, under-rated - oversees top a'
   town . . . Tawn 'all . . . an'th Market Place!
Ah! The Market . . . where cheerful dialect can still be heard -
'Ey Up Mi Duck' . . . a welcome: warm and still, happily, commonplace:
News and views expressed . . . though not always fully
   understood when with puzzled visitors shared!

Bath Street belies it's name: The old Open Air pool and
   Rutland Spa both long since demolished.
The Havelock and the beloved, Dew Drop Inn are no more
Others remain - but it's not the same . . . Too modern and polished!
The town and it's unique character will live on.
The Ritz and Scala Cinema buildings remain:
Kings and New Theatre have gone.
Modern developments and industries that we could not foresee,
   will thrive - and a new generation inspire.
Three railway stations once served the town. All were closed . . .
But now - a new one to use, and admire!

Bennerley Viaduct . . . A Rare 'forgotten' Masterpiece - also restored -

Towers over the School Playing Fields where many a goal I scored!

Oh the joy of those childhood years . . .

The sound of that dialect to my ears . . .

Ilson - perhaps an understated gem . . .

Ilkeston . . . My Ilkeston - 'Carpe Diem'!

ILSON LAD

When asked from whence I come . . .

"Derbyshire!". . . promptly, proudly, is the reply my enquirer will receive.

"Ah!". . . And immediately I see in my questioner's eye - Their vision . . .
    The beautiful images they perceive . . .

The Peak . . . The Dales . . . those beautiful views. The eyes never lie!

And rightly so . . . Derbyshire is a wonderful, special place.

I am proud of my county . . . no other can compare.

From Ancient, pre Roman times to present day . . . it has set the pace.

Innovation from Arkwright, Boulton to Royce . . . Challenge if you dare!

But now it's more the Peak - White or Dark which attracts.

To so many, a fondly remembered holiday or visit recalled.

Such, that now the mere mention of its name - the memory interacts.

However, not all of my county is beautiful and stone walled!

For I am an Ilson lad. Coal mines and ironworks everywhere once seen
    But there was woodland too - between the pits and fiery furnaces.

A childhood of priceless memories amidst that industrial scene.

Now a wistful look . . . Little evidence today of those old, ugly places.

Ilkeston . . . changed . . . is ever changing and yet still . . . quintessential.

A very special dialect that can still be heard: Danelaw based.

"Ey up mi duck" - Such a warm, friendly welcome . . . Very special.

Sure to be heard on Market Day . . . and most others . . .

Such nostalgia and happy memories interlaced.

So, Derbyshire - not all scenery and picture postcard views.

A county of which I am justly proud: Though exiled now.

I love that look when I declare that I'm Derbyshire bred . . . ' Cues . . .

An instant recall, an association: Envy . . . The eyes always avow!

NB

'Ilson' - Local dialect pronunciation of Ilkeston

ILISON LAD - BORN AND BRED

"Ey up mi duck!"

Oh what memories of childhood and home this greeting awakes!

Saturday morning: Ilkeston Market . . . I'm certain to hear the phrase.

That greeting . . . 'Ey up mi Duck'! My visit . . . my day it makes.

I smile . . . my spirits raise.

I visit less now . . . but feel at home when that greeting first meets my ears!

Happy memories . . . Nostalgia: those happy, formative years!

Fondly remembered - with great Pride.

In this world of political correctness, the plain, and the infuriatingly inane —

    long may this unique dialect remain.

A greeting which portrays much warmth, a welcome . . .

'though perhaps sadly betraying the passing days . . .

Of coal mining, ironworks and hosiery: Of childhood . . .

Much has changed - but the memories and happiness stays.

Notes

ILKESTON MARKET PLACE

Seated by the wall of St Mary's Church I gaze on a familiar scene . . .
Ilkeston Market Place.
The late summer's sun - warm on my face, highlights a surprisingly
Continental air to my view.
Now traffic free, the Market's surrounding buildings are more clearly seen.
I appraise the scene anew . . .
Some, their features part obscured by verdant leafy trees . . .
Others, dominant - striking - their profiles clearly defined . . .
What an array . . . and what History they portray.

The Market Place spreads sunlit, piazza like before me . . .
Overlooked by the castellated facade of the Town Hall -
Complete with balcony from which the Mayor could address all!
Built in 1866 Restored 1974 . . .
Dominant: Classical, stern Victorian symmetry.

Just visible to the right - Scala Cinema - and what a delight!
A Decorated terra cotta Edwardian Picture House built 1913
The second oldest in the country . . . Listed . . . it must be seen!
Its bright, ornate facade attracts . . . welcomes . . .
Restored: And it still shows films every night!

Adjacent . . . a small arc of colourful Maple tree
offers seating and shade which serves - complements
the Town's renowned cast iron fountain . . .
Its water supplied much earlier rustic settlements.
Now, the featured sirens - different visitors see.
Sixteenth century Taverns still jostle in that quaint corner
Ale, not water, the later travellers quest beneath the fauna!

Close by this reminder of the town's earlier history . . .
A striking example of Art Deco frontage . . .
Was for decades the Co-Op, but no longer so
The origins of the block something of a mystery . . .
Out of sight but close to hand - the Ritz Cinema
A classic example of the genre . . . Do not forgo!

On the southern aspect of the Market the - Cenotaph . . .
Dedicated to the Sherwood Foresters who died in the wars.
A traditional dour granite Monument - with appropriate epitaph -
Stands proudly afront the 'Carnegie Library' . . .
an impressive, imposing Listed Building
It's features now part hidden . . .
by a row of majestic trees notwithstanding!

The church in front of which I sit dates from the twelfth century
Although the present build is of post fire paternity . . .
'Tilchestune' itself is Domesday Book listed
Much then in which to be interested!
The current Market Place was up dated in 1993 -
Becoming largely Traffic Free . . .
But the 'Market' function dates back to 1252 . . .
Much before that recent review!
All this and more . . .
But with that . . . I will end my Market Tour.

DERBYSHIRE BEST

From dark, satanic hills - through Smedley's and Arkwright's early mills
From Roman times to Boulton, Royce, Rolls and the rest . . .
Derbyshire, pre-eminent, innovative and best!

From barren heights atop Snake Pass
To Kinderscout - scene of The Great Trespass . . .
From Ladybower's awesome presence
To Buxton's elegant, regal crescents.
From Black Peak and White Peak
To Bakewell - where puddings and tarts we seek.
From Chatsworth's majestic house and grounds To Walton's Dovedale -
Beauty and evocative sounds.
From Thorpe Cloud and Ashbourne's mineral water
To Derby's newly, restored Cathedral Quarter.
Hathersage, Wirksworth, Matlock and Eyam . . .
Each its own character, history and esteem.
From mines which yielded lead, iron, coal and more To meadows, Dales
and "shivering" Mam Tor . . .
Whatever the age - whatever the need
Derbyshire has planted and nurtured the seed.
From Ancient History and Blue John Mine, The Industrial Revolution,
Mills and the rest . . .
Derbyshire - pre-eminent, innovative, beautiful and still the best!

Notes

EY UP ME DUCK

Well . . . Thas cum t' Ilson . . .
Hast tha bin afore or i'st on aldee?
Up t' press . . . things may seem odd I dos say.
Ne'er mind . . . Yuh 's goalot to lon -
But dunna wittle: Let me lon yer . . .

Fost - They's found a reet gem!
See as much 'orrit as yer ken.

Nah . . . are yuh 'arkin?
Let's be raight . . .
Thay must visit market at top o' tahn . . .
ant' . . . museum whilst thase theire.
Aye . . . an' dunna forget to sae Scala cinema an 'all . . .
Anth Ritz if it's still thia . . . Art Deco . . . Gleg a look!

Victoria Park is well woth a stroll . . .
An' a walk up th' cut past Nutbrook
Brings yer to Shipley 'all -
   famed in that . . . Chatterley book.

Thay'll ah no trouble findin' a place fora drink . . .
More than thotty pubs - an' then lots more -
I seem to think . . .
But eatin' . . . that could be bit tricky
Unless it's fish an' chips - or sum other quickie . . .

Any rode I best be lettin' thee goo . . .
Otherwise I'm be yacking all th' day!
Hope you enjoy thee stay . . .
'Dew Drop' in agin if tha's out this way!.

Notes

EVOCATION

A wonderful, blissful summer morning - pleasantly warm.
I sit and revel in the beauty of the scene before me.
The grass is warm . . . recently shorn.
Derbyshire . . . glorious countryside . . . the magical, incomparable love . . .
One happy, contented me!
Ah! Yes . . . the River Dove . . . renowned, immortalised by Walton's prose
Tumbling, sparkling - reflecting the sunlight as it flows.

I see an angler - midstream, little more than knee deep. Waders and all.
I am part envious, part in awe as he fishes such a prime, magical stream.
Transposed - I dream of earlier days:
My youth, I recall.
But to return, to the moment. To my current theme!

His rod rises, flexes and then sweeps forward . . . slowly . . . gracefully.
His action, to me, brings to mind an orchestral conductor in mid melody . . .
At a distance I cannot see the anglers line . . . but it arcs, lands gently . . .
Smetana? Ma Vlast? Too contrived . . . Perhaps Mozart or, Tchaikovsky?

He rests now . . . the angle of the rod low to the rivers flow.
Eyes searching. His concentration is apparent.
Oblivious to the beauty of the scene.
Moving stealthily, he resumes the slow, smooth action of careful casting
What is he thinking? What is his scheme?
Clearly he is detached from cares and worries of life away from the stream.

Again - his preparations end. The rod flexes . . . I imagine the line arcing,
to land gently, so . . . gently.
Perhaps he has seen a ripple, some movement, some evidence of trout.
Slowly, gracefully . . .
I am lulled . . . I join him - if only in mind:
Tranquility. A timeless, seemingly silent ritual.
Is this what it is all about?

I am drawn into his world . . . Detached from whatever cares and stresses.
The day is magical. A world of calm, of beauty. Peace . . . Sublime!
The sun shines, the gentle breeze caresses.
I watch, I remember, I dream . . . Oblivious of time.
Time in which all my ills and worries appear to scatter . . .
How long did I watch? Minutes? Hours? Who knows?
Does it really matter?

THE POND

Two benches beneath the ancient, gnarled Hornbeam tree
    provide rest for those who merely come to see.
Mothers, with pushchairs and small children in tow, their knowledge of
    the ducks and nature bestow . . .
Willow trees on the eastern bank, cascade and shade.
Reeds: green, abundant, sway- the shallow pond invade
    allow pond life to rest, to feed and perhaps in Spring - to nest.
Ah . . . Spring . . . our pond at its beautiful, restful best.

The seasons each to their own, transpose our treasured pond.
Spring - vibrant and bright heralds Summer - another daily delight.
Lush: Shaded and cool . . . respite from the sun's fierce heat.
A haven of peace where family, friends and lovers meet.

Autumn - 'Season of mists and mellow fruitfulness'? No less!
Our pond exchanges its verdant green for glorious sunlit gold.
We walk with fallen leaves under foot . . . still beauty to behold.
Ducks dabble and delight: The days shorten: Betoken cold.

Winter - Gaunt and bleak? Not really so . . . but a difference seen!
The Hornbeam towers over a muted, less colourful view.
The water, agitated by blustery winds, takes on a darker hue . . .
Ducks remain . . . much the same.
Nature resting . . . another year to renew.

Notes

SEASONS

Autumn: Gone the golden days of 'Mellow Fruitfulness'
Now shorter days -misty days.
The sombre, slate grey skies of the subsiding Autumn season Obscured by
   cloud . . . so little chance of catching the sun's fading rays.
Nature prepares and with good reason . . .
Winter waits.

Winter: Of Discontent? Cold, icy, bleak . . .
Nature, and perhaps the mind, in seasonal hibernation.
The 'New Year' brings resolve and perhaps some Festive Cheer.
Occasionally the low Winter sun casts a brilliant, ethereal illumination.
Trees in leafless pose present a striking, stark silhouette.
But,soon buds will appear . . .
Spring is near!

Spring: So much more than 'Darling Buds . . .' Nature awakes.
Fresh, lush plants and flowers of wondrous multi-coloured hue.
Crystal clear sunlight highlights gardens, pasture and lakes.
A cornucopia of flower, fruit and corn. A beautiful vibrant view . . .
Summer to preview!

Summer: What more lovely and more temperate season could one ask?
Newly mown grass evokes pleasant memories of summers past.
Birds sing, bees buzz; as we, in summer sunshine bask.
Long, languid, blissful days ease into musk scented dusk.
Oh that this happy, joyous season could last and last.

Notes

THE GARDEN

Winter: The garden - grey, drear, forlorn . . .

Little colour save for the faded green of the uncut lawn The days short
and bleak . . .

Two trees, leafless . . . their branches like icy fingers, the limited light seek.

I remember forty nine and sixty three . . .

Winters like those, perhaps, we are now unlikely to see.

But - February brings early signs of Spring . . .

And the colours it will shortly bring.

Soon Snowdrops, crocus, daffodils will dance in the sun's pale rays . . .

Heralding, longer, warmer, sunlit days.

Mother Nature never ceases to amaze

As she unfolds her glorious, mysterious ways.

Notes

AUTUMN

Autumn . . . 'Season of mellow fruitfulness'

But . . . October - a felicitous month.

Perhaps the trees and flowers their summer splendour retain –

　Continue to delight - our joy and happiness maintain.

The days shorten, are cooler . . . the sun sinks early But what

　wonderful,spectacular sunsets it can display.

Red skies betoken yet another golden day.

Bees and birds still active - add joy to this magical scene.

But . . . eventually Nature takes her course . . .

Flowers droop, colours fade . . . not as vibrant as they

　once had been.

Lawns become forlorn . . . grasses turn an Autumnal fawn.

But all is not dismay - there are fruits and berries still to purloin!

And the sparkle of that first, frosty dawn . . .

Felicitous - yes. Mellow - yes.

But unrivalled in fruitfulness and . . .

New life will soon be born

Notes

SNOW

I wake! A strange stillness . . . silence.

The room is dark, save for the diffused light through the curtained window.

I listen . . . Nothing.

A strange stillness . . . Silence.

I lie . . . listen . . . There should be some sound I know . . .

I go to the window . . . Look . . . and there it is - Snow!

I look. The familiar view has gone.

The lawn, the edging, the flower bed, the path.

The avenue - not defined . . . Everything apparently . . . gone!

All replaced by an unblemished, contour - less, blanket of snow.

I am excited: I anticipate the morning view - illuminated

   by the low winter sun's glow.

I rise later. The day begins. The view . . . pristine - unchanged.

The undisturbed snow. A muffled, muted silence. Beauty.

But, my joy nor this magical scene - will remain unchanged.

People trudge, cars slip and skid. Life must go on . . .

Later children play . . . slide and snowmen build.

Soon the snow, like the beauty and my joy - will melt . . . be gone.

Notes

REMINISCENCE

The days, the weeks . . . months . . . even years - they come and they go.

  Time passes . . .

    Streams into rivers grow: Tides ebb and flow. Always have . . .

      and it will always be so.

      Memories too are much the same.

        Images, Dreams . . .

          They come and they go.

           May be vivid - or only half remembered schemes.

           Some happy - some sad . . .

           Some fleeting . . .

           Others remain.

            They recall a scene . . .

              Perhaps, too often now - seen as a case of

              'What mighthave been . . .'

              Easy to reminisce of all those scenes.

             Of those we miss . . .

            A look, a hug, a kiss -

             Fleeting - but bliss . . . sheer bliss

             Remembered . . .

              and it will always be so.

Notes

THE RIVER

As though embarrassed . . . shy and unsure . . .
A gentle, almost unnoticed bubbling.
The spring: for want of a description, emerges.
Bubbles and sparkles in the early morning light.
The sun's refactored rays add to this beautiful sight.
Tumbling playfully - the water forms rivulets - Each a sparkling,
    beautiful gentle flow seeking its way to the grassy slopes below.
Some merge and grow . . . create a more defined course
    But quite slow, gentle . . . no indication yet of its ultimate force.

Through lush green meadow, past brambles and thorn
    The waters may be hid from view though growing more sedate:
    clear . . . murmuring, meandering.
Habitat for flitting ephemera and busy, buzzing bee . . .
Breaking from the leafy canopy, a new approaching vista to see.

Now, fed by other streams, outfall and rain It has grown . . .
    Graceful? Gurgling? Mere periods from its past!
Now flowing, with pride and purpose, its humble beginnings cast -
    the river runs regally through ever changing, urban townscape
    offering peace, tranquility to inhabitants who wish the sprawl to escape.

Approaching its ultimate goal the river is majestic, all powerful.
A route-way to which road and rail, for ease of construction, are drawn.
Provider of power, of energy, of heating, of cooling for
the Industrial dawn.
    Perhaps an unwitting, unwilling threat of damage, of flood.
But, overall on its journey to the sea - a source of beauty,
    of delight and livelihood.

Notes

TIME AND TIDE . . .

"Time and tides wait for no one . . ."

Time marches inexorably on.

Tides ebb and flow -

As it has always been . . . and will ever be so.

Time is measurable, unchanging wherever we go.

Though it can appear to travel too quickly . . . or be so slow!

Time marches inexorably on.

Tides have seasons controlled by moon and sun . . .

Affecting us all -whatever has to be done.

Time marches inexorably on.

So how does time pass so quickly when deadlines near:

But slowly, oh so slowly, when our thoughts to a special treat veer?

Time marches inexorably on . . .

Notes

THE BALLET DANCER

S
She
Solo
Slim
Stylish
Silent
Sinuous
Special ...
Sylphlike.
Spiritual ... Serious.
Surreal ... Spectacular.
Sensational ... Sophisticated ... Special.
Secular Siren ...
Seductive Sprite ...
Slightly surreal ...
Smouldering Shakespearean symbolist.
Stylish shadowy silhouette ... Studious.
Sorrowful? Smiling? Selfless?
Slightly surreal ...
She ... Singular.
Searching ...
Sensitive.
Special.
Sublime.
Sinuous
Silent
Stylish.
Slim
Solo
She ...
Simply Sublime

Sublime ...
A
R
T

Notes

BALLET

She stands, silently, statuesque - 'En Pointe'

The music begins . . . Tchaikovsky? . . .

Could there be anything better?

Music, movement exquisitely combined.

Slowly, gracefully she moves.

Nothing but this 'Pas Seul' on my mind . . .

Well . . . yes -

The whole mesmeric, magical scene.

Where else can such grace and beauty be defined?

Where else this fusion of music and movement be seen?

She is supple, serene . . .

Divine! A dream to which I can only aspire

The Music, the Dance - enhance the scene . . .

Music and Movement . . . Love?

The combinations I can only admire

Supreme, sensuous . . .

Ultimate Art.

Notes

ART NOUVEAU

Oh! How little we really know of Art Nouveau . . .

Mackintosh, Morris, Klimt, Glasgow . . . Vienna?

Where did it start? Was it merely the 'Art'?

Or was it an inevitable reaction?

A genuine renaissance . . . or merely rejection of repression?

One and the same?

A term, a style . . . or a dissatisfaction?

Whichever, whatever . . . we are all of us, the recipients of its pleasure

    Architecture . . . Decorative Art . . . Design, Furniture . . .

Motifs . . . All 'New' to delight, inspire . . . and to Treasure.

Notes

THE KISS

'The Kiss . . .' Two words but myriad images ignited.

The mind . . . the memory - instantly excited.

Klimpt's warm, colourful portrayal . . . complex. but what do you see?

Rodin's sculpture - altogether cooler . . .

but less sublime would you agree?

The Kiss . . . Words which conjure and revive memories past . . .

Why so readily remembered? Why do these selected images last?

Why do some still bring a smile, a warm happy glow . . .

And others that recall . . . well only you can know!

That kiss . . . that one amongst so many, remains.and always will.

Why so different that you remember and still recall the thrill?

'The Kiss': more than contrasting forms of what we refer to as 'Art'

A memory . . . complex . . . complete . . . even if tinged with regret . . .

That moment will never depart.

STILL LIFE

She lies . . . No! More correctly . . . she reclines . . .
Her pose, the angles, the light - her best features define.
Still! Still, so still . . . no movement do I discern.
But she, though beautiful, is not my concern.

The others . . . Students, pupils, artists . . . call them what you will
Shuffle, squint, lean, incline their head - their aims to fulfil.
Their Tutor moves amongst them pointing, nodding . . .
perhaps in agreement . . . perhaps in doubt.
Whatever . . . They know. They know what it's all about.

Still Life! A structured, established, exacting Art Form.
With tutoring, practice, experience they will, in time, conform or,
reform.
But me? Life is much more unsure, surreal, veiled in mystery.
Changing, evolving: Never - 'Still'. The Holy Grail of confusing history.

Time passes and they have images to show . . . to share.
Even a hint of Cubism from those who dare!
Unfinished perhaps - fulfilment and satisfaction yet to find?
But . . . still she reclines . . . still so still. I wonder what is in her mind?

Me? Nothing to show. No clearer in what it is I endlessly pursue
Still Life . . . I can understand but. Life . . . I can still misconstrue . . .
Her beauty though I will treasure, remember . . . Art in human form.
And Life? Like the students . . . do I conform or . . . reform?

Notes

MATERIAL WORLD

Mondrian, Calder, Hepworth, Van Meure . . .

All around me a bewildering array of confusion, of hype!

Materials in profusion - metals, wood . . . even knotted human hair!

Displays . . . Collages . . . Constructed art of every conceivable type.

My senses, overwhelmed, recoil . . . is this serious, genuine? Do I care?

Confusion continues . . . Bewilderment . . . Chaos!

Then my 'Eureka' moment . . . Distant . . . but I see it!

Steel? Aluminium? Alloy? . . . Polished - burnished, bright.

Sense in a seemingly senseless world - Form, Function, Subjunction . . .

Solid, towering - a truly impressive . . . welcome sight!

Stunning and yet practical - Clarity of function.

Excitedly I approach this imposing, redeeming discovery.

Crowds are revelling in the ease, the simplicity of its use.

Simple to comprehend - its movement - simply up and down.

But their actions surely border on abuse . . .?

I stare, in dismay, in disbelief . . . and frown.

Then I realise . . . It's . . . the elevator . . . not an exhibit at all!

Embarrassed, shamefacedly I ascend on the elevator and exit the Hall

Notes

TWILIGHT

Twilight - a beautiful, soft gentle fading light . . .
    transition to darkness and night.
Twilight the precursor of sleep:
Dreams . . . Scenes . . . Schemes . . .
and 'What might have beens'.

Dreams: Memories of happy days.
Childhood, Family holidays . . . fun and games -
    some clearly remembered . . . some lost in a misty haze.
Scenes . . . Vivid recall of sights and events which gave delight . . .
Success much enjoyed -
and now - a much treasured respite.

Schemes: Oh those wonderful ideas . . .
Fabulous, elaborate . . . the foolproof plans - which sadly
    changed and now? Disappeared like quicksands.
What might of been? Nostalgic trips . . .
Perhaps the ultimate reverie.
Oft re-visited but oft, tending towards enhanced memory!

Twilight - Magical moments: Peaceful.
Prelude to sleep - Perchance to dream . . ..

Notes

IF MUSIC BE THE FOOD OF LOVE

"If music be the food of love, play on: Give me excess of it . . ."
Brilliant Beethoven . . . Brahms, melodious Mendelssohn.
Towering, thrilling, tormented Tchaikovsky
Sublime Sibelius, Chopin and of course, Mozart . . .
Great artists in their field, leaders of their Art.

My appetite for their serene sounds is difficult to satiate.
As I write . . . they sustain me . . . as I rest . . . as I contemplate . . .
My mood will dictate my musical need
Their vast repertoire will, my composing feed . . .

"Music soothes the savage breast . . ." another borrowed quote . . .
But now perhaps my writing is less aggressive . . . takes note.
More philosophical, more introspective . . . Less depressive:
Then feed me more . . . It's affect . . . stimulating and impressive!

Notes

Sunset with Sibelius

Red sky at night . . .

No: Not so much red, much more . . . cerise.

A gloriously hued canvas for a solitary, white cirrus cloud.

The scene brings peace and solace at the end of my day.

I gaze and feel a wonderful sense of calm .

The gentle strains of Sibelius bring to mind vistas . . .

of silver birch and pine.

The light slowly fades . . .

Slowly night descends.

Slowly . . . softly . . . Serene in the extreme.

His second symphony . . .

The soaring , slow second movement. - Sublime.

"If music be the food of love . . ."

My dreams begin . . . My day ends.

Soothing, satisfying, serenity sweeps over me.

The perfect end to the day.

"Sleep . . . sleep . . . Perchance to dream!"

Notes

THE EVENING SKY

A miscellany of fluffy clouds . . . abstract shapes.

Tinged a glorious range of reddish hues by the setting sun:

Contrasting with the clear, fading back drop of the evening sky.

Another wonderful summer day is run.

The view from my study window . . . framed as if a work of art brings a
feeling of calm and tranquility.

I sit . . . selected music playing softly . . .

By choice . . . a gentle opus by Mozart.

Wispy clouds silently drift - their format - less defined.

The sun slips silently from view . . . 'Goodnight dear heart'.

Then - almost indiscernible against the twilight sky Stars bedeck my
infinite canvas: Randomly aligned.

The night sky now gloriously lit by the moon on high.

The sky - through my window; my canvas; my Art.

STUDY-WINDOW ART

Notes

THE LAUNCH

My study window frames the evening summer sky -

Framed as though a work of Art.

Tonight the sky is clear - a beautiful cerise tinge

Save for a solitary, towering white cloud -

Much like a Wyoming desert dust twister - but benign.

Silent . . . spectacular and seemingly stationary.

A glorious, peaceful, tranquil composition.

Nature's contribution to my personal Gallery.

Glass in hand I relax . . . I reflect:

Music as often, complements my mellow mood.

Tonight a Beethoven Sonata . . . Appassionata.

The cloud gently fades leaving a clear, vaguely blush canvas.

Reverie . . . I treasure my priceless picture . . .

The evening . . . The peace and relaxation

Which Music and Art bestows.

AZURE

Again, as last night, my Study Window is a canvas . . . is priceless Art.

The day's blue sky . . . now less intense: Azure.

A thin veil of cloud . . . complementing, adding allure.

Contemporary in style; and yet . . .

The mind's images kick start.

Nothing discernible - Abstract . . . and then . . . soon depart.

As ever the visual picture evolves:

Light fades. Cue some Mozart.

The colours fade . . . wisps of cloud lost as colours merge.

Grey? No! Not worthy of the evenings vista: Argent . . .

Special . . . "the colour of her hair."

The still, sheer beauty of my tranquil, beautiful canvas . . .

Contentment complemented by Mozart's choral genius -

The closing chorus of the Requiem:

Ephemeral, Essorant Delicious!

Notes

ROSE

The early Spring day draws to its close . . .

Some time since I sat, blind undrawn, the evening sky to expose.

The setting sun casts a glorious, artistic rosy hue . . .

Mondrian comes to mind . . . Shades . . . A glorious view.

Abstract, and yet . . . Shapes appear, dissolve, fade - re -appear . . .

Darkness removes the colour, the glow - but not the panacea.

Movement, swift, silent catches my eye . . .

Bats swooping silently, vaguely discernible against the night sky.

An added dimension to my canvas. Delight!

The first viewing of the year.

How appropriate that Mozart's Eine Kline Nachtmusik softly plays.

My turbulent, repressive period melts under this magical scene.

Soothing sounds . . . A calming canvas. Where have I been?

Art, Music, Poetry restore belief . . . the senses . . .

   the comfort of routine.

Notes

AMBER

Tonight . . . What an amazing light and resultant, back-lit sight!

The equal of the finest skyscapes by the great Masters.

Cirrus wisps refract the setting amber glow . . .

This surely is the Masterpiece of the show.

The gusty winds which cooled the day have died . . .

Resulting in the glorious coloured tableau I see.

A dramatic, vibrant tapestry to which my words seem bland.

Constable, Turner, Van Gogh?

A joyous wonderland.

I am transposed, energised by this aerial display.

What music can complement this sumptuous, golden scene?

Perhaps Rimsky-Korsakov?

I am drawn towards sumptuous, expansive - Scheherazade.

Warm, romantic . . . Supreme.

But as this peerless show dissolves . . . Twilight evolves.

Peace, tranquility . . . Mendelssohn - 'Midsummer Nights Dream'?

Notes

REVERIE

Rather strange today . . . blustery showers . . . thunder and stormy

winds punctuate the recent oppressive - hot, humidity.

But tonight a calm, quiet tranquility.

The tumultuous thunder clouds fade to reveal an expansive clear sky . . .

Defining the beauty:

The colour - defeats me . . . Why?

A motionless canvas - a peaceful, silent bliss.

My mind . . . unbidden . . . recalls that kiss.

Reverie . . . a divine, dreamlike, timeless trance . . .

No need tonight for music, this joy to enhance.

A wonderful, though now - distant memory . . .

That daylight colour disappears - Day becomes night -

A thoughtful, unaccompanied - silent reverie.

CLOSURE

May: But what a day!

Rain . . . and more of the same.

This evening torrents of rain obscure my window pane.

No view . . . No canvas on display,

A grey, cheerless day. Dismay. What more to say

The same countrywide: "Rain Stopped Play"!

With no visual distraction I need music to lift the gloom.

Beethoven's Seventh Symphony fills the room . . .

"Apotheosis of the Dance". . . Wagner did decree . . .

Who am I to disagree?

The evening passes - Darkness falls.

"And so to bed"

"To sleep, to sleep . . . perchance to dream . . ."

Both oft misquoted, both misconstrued . . .

"Tomorrow is another day . . ." As is said . . . and . . .

It will still be May! That "Merry Month" Oh . . .

"Rain, rain go away. Come again . . . Another day"!

Notes

EIGHTY

I'm eighty today . . .

Perhaps I have said most of what I have to say.

So, Poetry- take a back seat . . . perhaps another day!

It is sunny, warm and fine . . .

But Autumn weather is due in three days time.

The garden already shows that early sign.

A letter informs me that my State Pension is now increased - If . . .

    by the end of the month I am not 'Deceased'!

By anotherTwenty five pence per week my palm will be greased.

Now . . . IF I am a thrifty, careful guy . . .

By Christmas . . .

A joyful, Celebratory cup of coffee I will be able to buy!

EXTRA . . . EXTRA

A closing Extra!

For those who missed the earlier two anthologies of

'THIS ISNOT A CRICKET BOOK' trilogy . . .

I close with perhaps my favourite

'CONTEMPLATION'

Notes

CONTEMPLATION

I have a wooden garden bench - not grand enough to call a bower . . .

But, yes it is surrounded by bushes, wisteria and flower.

I use it as a sort of retreat where I rest and meditate.

Whilst I sit, I relax, think - and current issues contemplate.

I think about this, and that . . . sometimes the other . . .

And when I meditate . . . well one thing leads to another.

Perhaps the world really is flat -

But No! Satellites and science put pay to that.

Maybe the moon is made of cheese -

No, that's just a childish tease.

Does a cat have nine lives?

Or is that just an uttering of those 'Old Wives'?

A rainbow's end has a crock of gold . . .

But that's not true I've since been told.

Perhaps other, more important issues I should deliberate . . .

Politics, Religion, the meaning of life . . . on these I should concentrate.

But they really do not suit my contemplative, wistful mood . . .

That pleasantly relaxing, restorative quietude.

So my bench will remain - My personal, philosophical habitat . . .

Where I go to rest, meditate . . . and think of this and that!

ACKNOWLEDGEMENT

As a would-be writer, the composing of an acknowledgement should be routine . . .

However, the enormous contributions to the production of this Anthology by Deb Griffiths of Budding Authors Assistant cannot be overstated. Layout, Editing, Graphic Design (another outstanding Cover) are Deb's work. Without this input, my words would remain just words.

Many thanks!

Printed in Great Britain
by Amazon

67883285R00052